The Mallerstang Murder!

BY
Millie Aveyard

(Gilly Penworth Murder Investigations)

2015

Hello, Millie speaking, I need to speak to you urgently regarding both the Russian and Dutch Mafia Gangs. My gut feeling is that this is going to be one hell of an explosion and it will go in a direction that no one as mentioned before!

Although if you think about it the name of the person involved and the Village together with the Head of the whole Mafia Gangs, it really should have been thought about sooner!

Boys I think that we should put out a red alert, and I will tell you why; Toni is an out and out Italian Mafia Man, he was brought up that why by Ken and his own Mother's family. There is no question about that!

The Italian Mafia is Toni's family if you like with his Grandfather's,Uncles and his brothers all involved. But on the other hand he is having trouble with the Russian Mafia and the Dutch Mafia because the Russian Mafia is out to take over the cartels governed by the Dutch.

Very early this morning I received a tip off from someone I have not spoken to for a few years now, and he gave some one information regarding what Toni had been telling him as they came over from Italy! Now normally I would not believe everything but over the years I have learnt that when you are given information by this particular chap there is always some element within the rubbish of the real hard truth!

This particular member of the Government who I actually always call Benedict was at one time a member of the Government but eventually retired as he must be in his late seventies even early eighties by now!

He certainly comes over as a very likeable chap, and I am sure he would keep a party going, but you know at times you are being fed certain information as he would like you to do the dirty work and spread it around!

I now believe that the Russian Mafia and the Dutch Mafia are going to fight it out! I also believe that the Head of the Mafia Gangs, together with the Italian Mafia,and the Chinese Mafia,plus the Russian and Dutch Gangs, all operate in Scotland with a turnover of around £33 Billion!

Just think about all the various Mafia Gangs involved and a few more added on! Now this chap is willing to come down and meet with me, he will be on a train which comes into Yorkshire but as I have already said I do not trust him so my home is completely out of bounds to him!

We could arrange for him to catch the train that comes down from Carlisle and he could then get off at the first station, I would suggest Skipton, then we could have a coffee with him and see what he would like to tell me!

What do you think, and would you attend with me? Take his mobile number and ask him if he is willing to meet with me in Skipton. The Number is 079567333589. Whatever you do, please do not let him know where we are living; he would sell the information for millions!

Don't worry we will certainly speak direct to him, also he will be told that any meeting will involve both of us plus you! Thank you. One more thing, try and get the meeting for tomorrow!

Millie, yes boys your late, what time is it? about 8.30p.m. Listen Millie your chap sounded a little strange shall we say, as if he thought he was being followed! Well knowing what I do about him and what he has carried out over the years, everyone and their dog could be stalking him! He is not a good person by any stretch of the imagination! He is vindictive, cruel,nasty, and the murders he as been instrumental in carrying out is no one's business!

If you think he carried out 250 murders during his working life add a further couple of thousand at least and you might be some where in the region but not very close! He is an evil man but as been made that way by the various people within Whitehall who needed certain things to take place. The only person who was guaranteed to get the job done was this Chap!

Well, we have to act now, so if you can contact him and arrange a time when he will be in Skipton we will work to that!

Let me know as soon as you have spoken with him! But just be careful as he is devious by any stretch of the imagination!

Gilly, Millie speaking, can you talk or do you have

someone with you? Just give me time to take my dogs out of the car, and I will 'phone you back! Yes OK, but hurry because I want you in on a case I have!

Boys are you hearing me, only softly I would say you have a problem on the line, leave it with you boys! Millie one thing not Skipton at any price! Why? Don't know,but settle it as more tea places!

Millie, someone as tried to patch your line! How can they when it all comes via you! Good question Millie, but they have and the only way they can,is if they work like us! Now it certainly is not this end, so who do we know, that would know of our location and the numbers we are operating with? Once we know the answer to that we have the person who is trying to stop us from working with you Millie!

Well there is me and my husband, there are your girlfriends and you two, and no one else as far as I can see!also my young daughters!

Now we have the worry about meeting this chap, someone down south boys, oh yes it is! This is not the first time in my lifetime, they have tried this before on occasions! But I no longer have my Professor Hall active, he retired due to ill health! Right well I will go direct to the Prime Minister and see what I get back!plus will get Prof. to have a word with them, that still works!

Just never forget they could have been bought down south, it certainly would not be the first time, would it!

I remember when Professor Hall and I had to sort the whole Mafia Gangs out of Westminster, and they were actually giving monies to all the clerical staff in Whitehall and even the people in the Prime Ministers Office were being given cash backhanders from the Mafia!

It was just like being on the set of a second rate Film about Mafia Gangs, I have never seen so much Cash monies banded around and all the staff from the Office Boy to the Prime Minister's Office were taking the money! Totally unbelievable and this had been going on for a good few years!

Hello Millie, gosh you are difficult to get hold of Gilly! what are you talking about, and why use this mobile? Because there is a message on the other two lines and even the patched one, saying due to a death within your family you will not be taking calls for sometime and to try the mobile if the matter is urgent!

OH my God! This is getting worse! Gilly I had and still have a large job for you but I am not sure I should ask you to do it, as there is something bad afoot, as I see it now! All the "secret" lines are down therefore not secret at all!

Also our Mothers would never forgive me if anything happened to you! If I allowed my young Cousin to be involved in the twilight dealings of murders by the Mafia Gangs! Those two together would be worse than all the Mafia Gangs put together!

Hello Boys, why are you using your mobile to our mobile? Simple all my phones and yours have been taken over by the Mafia I would presume! Don't be silly Millie, I kid you not but someone some how as broken through security of Westminster and there is going to be one hell of a fall out with this lot!

Right , Millie we will come now to where you are and don't say where you are any more on any 'phone! Right you are, we are completely foxed, well I hope for all our sakes you work it out within the next hour or so!

Now Gilly do you wish to come over and talk about what I was giving you, yes I will make a room available as usual then you can bring your friends, OH that would be a good idea. I understand Millie!see you half an hour!

How can the Mafia break security? I don't believe it is the Mafia, but could it be someone who is close to Benedict and trying to find out what he is working on now? I think this stems from down South!

Hello boys, you look down but thank God not out! Have you found anything out? Not much but it could be that the CIA is involved! What! You must be having us on! Millie we think somehow for whatever reason Benedict is right in the middle of this, and that is why all this is taking place!
Whatever "this" is! Is due to the fact that you are having this meeting with Benedict in the morning, and probably why he would not think about Skipton but changed it to Settle!

That is one thing I do not understand, at least in Skipton

you can wonder around look in shop windows, whereas in Settle you will walk into the Market Place, and stand out dressed in the Westminster Suits! You would be spotted straight away!

    I have missed something in all of this, Gilly put your thinking cap on and take it from the start to where we are having a meeting in Settle with Benedict who is coming down from Scotland via Carlisle and should be meeting us in Settle at about 8a.m.! Probably a little after that depending if the train is delayed at Carlisle!

    Tell me more about this chap called Benedict, Millie and then I can have a mind view of him. Well Benedict was very well thought of in Government circles, but then they decided that he was too friendly with the Mafia Gangs, whether this was ever true or not, no one seems to know!

    I could certainly provide evidence that certain other people were shall we say extremely friendly with the large Mafia Gangs,but not sure about Benedict as I have never had proof of this!

    He was asked to leave the Government and the story given to the Newspapers was he retired due to ill health! Why he was singled out in the Government I have no idea, because I can certainly prove that there are far worse people than him who are still in Government, and I can provide evidence if required, with connections with the Leaders of all the Mafia Gangs! Including one who is related to the new Leader of all Mafia Gangs!

    Gilly, I am nearly asleep, I am off to bed, we have to be in Settle for 8a.m. Do you want to let the Dogs out again, no they will be ok now they were out about half an hour ago. Everyone else as gone up. Lets check all the windows and doors, and then we will go up as well!

    Right all clear Millie, see you in the morning, what time do we have to leave here? No later than 5.15am. Is it really worth going to bed one asks, get off with you! Night!

    Millie, I am leaving the dogs here for the rest of them, as they were restless during the night, and they are only like that if there is something outside! Right well My Phil is here and with your dogs and ours, and the boys and they are all armed I have to say! We should be OK!

Now Gilly do you wish to be armed, yes please can I have the usual one, yes here you are, and I have my two as usual.

What time do you make it Millie, nearly 5.30a.m. We should be in good time, as I do not think the traffic will be bad this morning! If it had been the Market Day it would be horrendous with all the various Cattle Trucks that park in the Market Place!

I will park in the Station and ask them if they know when the Carlisle Settle Train is due in, if it is a while yet, we may as well have some coffee! Stay in the car Gilly and keep an eye open for Benedict! Millie what ever is the matter, you look really upset? Do I? Well I asked the Inspector on the Platform over there about the timing for the Train. All he said was that there had been an accident on the line, and if I wanted to know more than that we would have to go out to Ribble Head!

I am going to call in the Police Station on our way, and just ask what is happening! You would have thought they would have given something over the tannoy! Not to worry hopefully the Police Station will know more of what is happening on the line!

Gilly are you coming into the Station with me? Yes, I think I should! Right lets go in! Good Morning I have been told to come here and ask about the Carlisle Train, which I am told as had an accident!

Well if you would like to sit down both of you in those chairs near the fire, I won't be long! Thank you, come on Gilly at least it is warm in here!

What do you think as happened Millie? Not sure really, but it must be very bad otherwise they would have been more forth coming! Don't you think so? Yes you are right Millie, I was just thinking that! They have either knocked someone down on a crossing or something like that!

There is definitely a Dead Body involved somehow! Just at this second I cannot bring to mind the lay-out of the Tracks/Lines call them what you will!

We will go back to the Car and drive up and see exactly what they are talking about, OK, but remember it could be a body we know!

Ladies, before you go are you expecting anyone on this Train? Yes I am, he is a retired Member of Parliament, retired some years ago now due to ill health! Can I ask you how old he is? Well not sure, but I would say 75 years plus to early eighties!

Right Ladies if I showed you a photograph which was taken this morning would you be able to recognise them? I would think so, well take a look at this photograph which was taken this morning, This chap was thrown off the Carlisle Train this morning! Now sit down and just take your time!

OH my God! I am sure that is Benedict; I am sorry I have never known his correct name, he worked for M16 years ago and I have always called him Benedict! Well Ladies this gentleman as been stabbed in the back, but not only that he was shot in the chest then thrown out of the Train Door! Pure out and out murder!

Have you any idea by whom this murder was carried out and when it was carried out? It was certainly carried out at 8am this morning! How very odd. He had an appointment to see me at 8.15am this morning. Benedict 'phoned me yesterday to ask if I could meet him in Settle, and not in Skipton as we had previously arranged. He fixed the Meeting in Skipton about three weeks ago, but yesterday he 'phoned me from Scotland no idea where he was in Scotland! He said he was coming down on the Carlisle Settle train and could I meet with him in Settle and not Skipton as he did not wish to go into Skipton!

It certainly makes you think that someone was tracking him, some how and that is why he cancelled meeting in Skipton!

I believe I can see a little of what might be taking place on the ground, I have not been party to any conversations regarding this, but because of what I do, and have done for a good number of years together with Professor Hall. I can make a qualified guess, and unfortunately I think I will be correct in what I am thinking!

Did you say Professor Hall, yes why? Because I have met him a few times, when we have had bodies around. Well in that case you have met me in the distant past too!

Now I would like you to make an urgent call to your Chief

Constable, tell him we need him to come urgently, give him my name and also say that I have asked Gilly Penworth (Murder)Investigations Ltd. To be involved in this matter. Your Chief Constable will like that!

    The Chief is on his way and says he will be here in half an hour, delighted that Gilly involved, and says he thinks you will have some idea of what as taken place or is taking place!

    Well with Benedict coming down from Scotland, and the way he was thrown from the Train and also a belt and braces Murder! No I will wait for the Chief Constable to arrive and then I will reveal what I think is taking place!

    In the meantime could I use your 'phone, the private 'phone please, how did you know about our Private 'phones? Because of whom I am and who I worked very closely with for years!

    Good afternoon, all of you especially Millie and Gilly! You should have been shown into my Office, I apologise for them keeping you in here, it was lovely a real fire! Well yes there is that, but there is also one in my Office!

    Now sit down both of you, would you like anything to drink, warm or cold? I think we would both life Coffee please, as we had quite a shock this morning, identifying by that photo poor Mr. Benedict!

    Now you have your coffee, and then tell me what you are thinking Millie, as I am sure you will have thought about it a great deal this morning! Yes I have, and it makes it even more complicated with this particular murder.

    Well Chief Constable you might not believe me, but I will tell you what I believe is happening and more to the point what will happen in the very near future. That is the worrying part of this whole plan!

    The Murder of Benedict was carried out on the instructions of the Head of all the Mafia Gangs! His name is Toni, with e request from his uncle Robertson-Fox;he was a lovely little boy but was soon groomed by his well known Father to be the Ruler one day of all the Mafia Cartels!

    I have to say he is very well respected amongst their own circles, he certainly is a chip off the old block! The one thing you must always remember is that no Mafia Gang takes prisoners! They just murder, it makes everything so clean and tidy!

Benedict was being tracked some how and that is why he must have cancelled his plan to meet in Skipton! I believe he must have gained some information regarding all the Mafia Gangs and wanted to let me know what was happening on the ground. Unfortunately someone on the train who must have been the one tracking him, shot and stabbed in whilst on the train, which made quite sure he could not inform me of anything that he had come across whilst in Scotland.

I firmly believe that the answer for this murder is buried in the depths of Scotland!amongst all the Mafia Cartels in Scotland! But I will come back to that in a second.

When Benedict was within the Government down in Whitehall, He was asked to concentrate solely on the Mafia Gangs all around the World, such as Italy,Russia, China,The Dutch, Mexico, Ireland,United States of America, in fact all of the small Mafia Gangs as well!

You will see that these Gangs are all controlled by one Leader, we have Toni now in full charge of all these various Gangs! But as you know the Mafia is the Mafia and they all pull together! A huge workforce I think you will agree!

Benedict had been very quiet, I have not been contacted by him either on the Patch nor by 'phone or documents for over two years now, until three weeks ago when he wanted to meet with me in Skipton! We arranged to meet and talk, unfortunately he never said why he wanted to talk! But then he always operated in this way! I never thought anything about it until this murder on the Train!

Benedict phoned me direct from Scotland the other day and said he did not wish to be seen in Skipton and he would be coming down on the Carlisle Settle train and would I meet him off the train in Settle, I said yes as I was curious as to why he wanted to meet in Skipton after all this time, and now even more curious as to the meeting arranged now in Settle because he did not wish to be seen in Skipton which I thought was most strange for him, he normally would be seen out and about anywhere!

Benedict 'phoned me the day before he caught the train down, and he wanted to talk but thought it was better to wait and speak to me direct!

Now please listen to all I have to say and then ask any questions you like, I will answer them all if I can!

I am sure as eggs are eggs that this murder as been carried out by the Mafia Gangs! Benedict phoned me from Scotland to arrange our Meeting in Skipton, which means to me that he was going to spill some rather interesting beans with regard to all the big players within the Mafia Cartels! I believe that after Benedict's visit to the Mafia Cartels in Scotland, a price had been put out for his Murder! That is why Benedict was shot and stabbed and thrown out of the Train!

Benedict's visit to Scotland I believe was in connection with all the various Mafia Gangs operating there! Were any of you aware that the biggest stream of monies for the Mafia Cartels is in Scotland, the Mafia Cartels in Scotland as a turnover of 33 Billion Pounds or perhaps I should say the Turnover in anyone year is worth 33 Billion Pounds!

I certainly cannot prove anything at the moment but I am sure that I am one hundred per cent correct in saying that Benedict's murder was carried out by the Head of all the Mafia Gangs, in other words by young Toni!

Benedict's murder as been used as a message to those watching, that you do not interfere with the Mafia Gangs, because if you do, you will be dealt with by murder! Perhaps I will receive more information during the morning, if not we will have to make our own enquiries regarding this particular murder!

In front of Benedict in Scotland he spoke of the Chinese Mafia, the Italian Mafia, into which Toni the Leader of all Mafia Gangs, was born into! The Russian Mafia, Dutch Mafia, the Mexico Mafia, the United State of America Mafia and the Irish Mafia!

All these Mafia Gangs were part and parcel of the massive turnover of 33 Billion Pounds per year just in Scotland! Just think what the turnover is for all around the World!

I believe that Toni sent this message to the British

Government, to make sure they knew it was carried out by the new Head of all the Mafia Gangs!Ken's son Toni!

Now we shall have some massive fall out from this murder! We shall certainly have to watch our backs even more than normal! Don't forget our 'phones had been tampered with yesterday, and now Benedict's murder this morning!

I am going to use the Police Phone again and try and contact the Black Suits and see if they have had a good day!

Gilly what I would like you to do is try and speak with someone down in Westminster, I will give you his name and telephone number, and do not be taken for a fool, because he is a devious person. You must start as you mean to go on, you must come over to him just like a school teacher, otherwise he will take you for a mug! No seriously he does it on purpose and then you end up having to make more 'phone calls, all of which are not necessary!

When I have finished with the Black Suits, try and 'phone this number you need the private phone and key in 008 then the patch will start then key in 1000. you should end up with the chap You must stress that we need four extra patch call lines, as the Mafia seem to have infiltrated some of our lines!

Then tell him to 'phone me on the mobile, do not give the number to him even if he does ask for it. They have the numbers make him work! Tell him all our lives are in danger because of the lack of our 'phones and those four together with the 'phones already in place require top priority from this second! As lives are in danger!

Do that, and then remember to give me your Contract which I will sign together with the Chief Constable, and then he will have something for you as well! We certainly will keep you busy for the next couple of years at least, but you should take some on board from the Chief Constable, as it will stand you in good stead for later!

Would like to take this work on Gilly, or am I being too pushy for you? No Millie you are just being you! I am very happy that you like to look out for me, and I need the work as you know, so don't stop just keep looking out for me as normal!

The question at the front of my mind is why suddenly did

Benedict want a meeting with me after two years, and why did he have to cancel Skipton, and why when he caught the train why was he given a belt and braces job!

I am sure that he had found out something regarding the Mafia Gangs in Scotland! For the life in me I cannot think it is to do just with Scotland, I think they all relate to each other!

Millie, you have just answered your own question! How did I answer it? Because think about it, in every Country all the Mafia Gangs are there? Yes that is correct, well if the yearly turnover for Scotland is turnover of 33 billion, just think what France, China, Spain, Italy, Greece, Turkey, United States of America.

I go all around the world, but just think what all that adds up to! Plus you have to add in Dutch Mafia and the Irish Mafia, all the players in the East, and little Islands dotted around the world! It is just so unbelievable!

I now believe that Benedict wanted to inform me about the Mafia Gangs on his journey back home from his meetings in Scotland! He obviously was going to inform me of all the intrigues within the Mafia Gangs, plus I think he would have warned me what Sir Marcus Henry Robertson-Fox was trying to make his own! That chap is one hell of a very nasty piece of work and I think he could have contacted the Mafia and asked them to remove Benedict coming down on the train from Scotland which would mean he could not have time to warn me!

Gilly, first case for you! Use your own patch line, it is up and running and when dealing with any of your own cases, use your own private lines, do not give your private line numbers out except to the Chief Constable and for the time being the family and MI6.

Oh and Gilly, I nearly forgot with all these comings and goings! You have your own MI6 contacts, you will find all the information in your top right hand drawer!

Gilly, please can you find out everything about Robertson-Fox, all the latest at Westminster both official and gossip, see if we can find out what Benedict knew about this chap! One more thing regarding both Robertson-Fox and also Benedict! Get the boys in black to look at the Bank Accounts for both of them, we need to see what has been paid into their accounts over the last six months!

Also ask the Boys to look and see if they have both paid hefty backhanders to anyone! You should be able to see if any payments have been made into the account by any of the Mafia Gangs and likewise if any payments have been paid to any of the Gangs! Millie is there anything else you need, yes as much evidence you can get both for Robertson-Fox and Benedict dealings with any of the Mafia Gangs!

Hello boys are you there, loud and clear Millie, first thing are our homes safe, yes Millie all of them! Plus everything working so far, there is so much equipment up and running it is like being in a Spaceship!

We have all the new equipment and various new telephone lines, plus all the equipment we had but could never use because of the lack of Office space, now we have all of that equipment plus all the new equipment!

Millie talking about our homes, the girls have been over the moon with what you did with the Houses. So much so that we are having a Double Wedding in the very near future and they wondered if you would allow your daughters to be Bridesmaids?

Well when you see my daughters ask them, I am sure they would love to be bridesmaids providing the dresses do not have to be Red, with bright Ginger hair they never wear red, blue and green are good colours for them, various shades will be good!. But Red is a no go area!

If the security is up and running, how did they manage last time to get into the security system, I am sure you will find out when your letter from Mr. Benedict arrives! How do you know Mr. Benedict? We don't know him Millie, but he came via the Patch, said he was down in Westminster, which he must have been to come in on the Patch!

Yes he was down in Westminster, but he has just been murdered by the Leader of the whole of the Mafia Gangs! He was in Scotland last week and 'phoned me, then was murdered on the Carlisle-Settle Train they shot and stabbed him! What I call a belt and braces job!

Well the message we received for you on the Patch was as follows "evil aspects of the Gangs being rolled forward! Don't trust anyone unless they are known to you and only then if it is on Patch! Or the Private Lines! If in any doubt check and double check! " Letter was posted to you, so it should arrive very soon!

Mr.Benedict said he had posted a letter to you because that was the only certain way to give information to you without other people reading it first!

Which means our mail is opened in Westminster first! Right boys,Just ask Westminster about all our mail, and ask point blank if our mail is always opened first by them!

When they say yes as they should, just play hell with them, make it really big! Create the biggest stink they have ever had!

Benedict was in his late Seventies early eighties, but he knew everything that goes on in Westminster! He was always full of good and trusted information, he certainly knew a lot of good influential people. He would try and help anyone and point them in the right direction!

I hope his letter explains what he wanted me to know on the last 'phone call he made from
Scotland last week!

Now we are up and running again Boys, we have a lot of investigations to move along, all due to the Mafia Gangs! Don't worry Millie we certainly have enough equipment to monitor the world!

Careful we said that last time, and look what happened, and when we moved back home! Yes we know Millie, but that was down purely to crooked people; not our equipment! So who was crooked then? You won't believe us Millie but a member of MI6, he was based in London, thank God we never met him, but he is now in Jail and will never be free again! He tried it at one of the Royal Palaces and that is where they caught him!

While I am on the line with you, you have met my cousin Gilly Penworth haven't you, Yes, she was involved in all those bodies buried in a garden, way back! Yes that is Gilly, I want her having her own **patched** lines and private phones, have they been given to her yet? I will check and make sure, but if they have not been switched on they certainly will be today I promise!

Well make sure they are done in the name of Gilly Penworth Murder Investigations, actually she as made it into a limited company, but just put it for Gilly Penworth Murder Investigations!She will be carrying out certain work for the Chief Constable as well as working with us!

Now the Chap I hold totally responsible for Benedict's Murder is well known in the halls of Westminster. He is Sir Marcus Henry Robertson-Fox! I managed to have evidence in writing regarding his dalliance with the Mafia Gangs, including all payments into his Private Bank Account from all the Mafia Gangs around the World!

Millie, I had to sign for this package and it was posted in Scotland, I am coming Gilly,just wait, let me see the handwriting please; yes it is certainly from Benedict! Well now hopefully we may know a little more about what the Mafia Gangs are intending to do!

Dear Millie,

I am sending this letter as well as the package, as I think you should be aware of the devious and evil person Sir Marcus Henry Robertson-Fox! Whatever you decide to do with this package; just take care and trust no one in Westminster!

I remember some while ago now, you managed to have evidence in writing regarding Robinson-Fox's connections with all the Mafia Gangs!

I enclose all the evidence I have collected over all the years regarding this person Robertson-Fox! I believe Robertson-Fox as found out about me having this knowledge about the Mafia and this chap Fox is certainly a sly Old Fox – excuse my Pun!

You will see Millie that I have enclosed his Bank Statements showing incoming payments from the various Mafia Gangs. Also he has another Private Account at the Top Private Bank in London, from that you will see that not only are the Mafia Gangs of Mexico and the United States paying large amounts of money into this Account on a monthly basis, as well as a trickle of smaller amounts from the Italian Mafia Gang!

    I presume you will not know this piece of information I am going to give you, but Robertson-Fox is the twin brother of Ken, the pathologist who left and joined into the family business! The Mafia Gangs! He is older than Ken by 7 minutes!
Just enough for him to take his Grandfather's Title, hence the Sir in front of his name!

    I know that Robertson-Fox thought he should be the next leader of all the Mafia Gangs, but Toni was Ken's Son and Ken had been the Leader, and his daughter after him, therefore Toni was granted the title of Leader of all Mafia Gangs!

    With regard to age Robertson-Fox is the slightly older twin by just 7 minutes but he still feels that the 7 minutes should make him the Leader of all Mafia Gangs!

    I certainly believe that if Robertson-Fox could see away of doing away with Toni by murder, which would not lead straight back to himself, then poor Toni would have been murdered months ago!

    I should tell you Millie that during my trip up to Scotland I have been followed by two MI6 Chaps who I thought had been sacked years ago, and that is why I could not meet with you in Skipton!

    Always make sure Millie who you are dealing with and keep safe. Just do not trust anyone from down in the South, especially in MI5! Yes I do mean MI5!

    Take care of yourself, and only trust the people you know well!

I firmly believe that by the time you receive this package and papers I shall have been murdered by MI6 but do not let them know about these papers until you have read them and you decide what to do about them! Do not let them bully you!

If I may suggest something to you, I know I have only met with Gilly once with regard to those bodies in the back garden, but she certainly works well; and not afraid to plough into the mess. Also as a good working relationship with the Chief Constable of your Area.

You can call me a fussy old chap but I will not hear you Millie, as I shall be dead already, murdered by the crooks in Westminster!

Allow Gilly to take on the case of looking into the background of Sir Marcus Henry Robertson-Fox, whilst you concentrate on the complete Mafia Gangs around the world!

As far as I understood the affairs in Scotland, there is going to be a massive explosion in that certain Gangs are under attack to be taken over by certain other parts of the Mafia. Keep your ear to the ground, as the Italian and Russian and Dutch and Irish Gangs are not happy! They could be crucial in the race for something to happen!

What will happen in all this turmoil is anyone's guess at the moment, but I would think within the next few weeks, all Hell will be let loose once more regarding these gangs, I only hope they will cool down later!

The one person at the top of the pile with regard to the Mafia Explosion will be Robertson-Fox, if he could be quietly murdered before that explosion takes place, then you should see things more or less return to normal.

I am not saying you should orchestrate a war within the Mafia Gangs but it certainly would not do any harm to you, and hopefully the first one to be murdered would be Robertson-Fox!

    Take care of your lovely family, and when you have a problem I hope you will say I wonder what Benedict would have done! and once you think of it, just do it!

    All the best Millie to you and all your family, sorry we could not meet again.

    Yours sincerely.

Benedict.

    What a lovely note to send me, but poor old Benedict he should not have had all that worry at his age! Well Boys, we know what we must do, do we Mille? Listen we have to make sure that any explosion of all the Mafia Gangs does not leave any debris on us!

    Gilly, another job for you and only use the Patch lines and the Private Phones from now on. Right we need up-to-date information regarding every Mafia Gang worldwide, it is a huge job Gilly but could be very well cost affective! Are you for the job Gilly? You bet I am!

    Gilly speak with your friend the Chief Constable and ask him where Benedict's body is and then we need to arrange him a church Funeral and could you organise flowers for the top of his coffin, please!

    Also Gilly could you ask the Chief Constable if he could make a discreet enquiry into whether Benedict as any living family, because I had the impression he was all alone. We need to organise a funeral for him this coming week!

    Right Millie, I will get on to that now, and come back when I have all the details, you are a help I have to say that! Is that all Millie? For now yes, Spurs are earned you know, not given! Cheeky devil! I heard that madam, you were meant to

Millie, yes I thought I was!

Do you like working with all of us Gilly, yes because I can bounce things off you, and yes I know we don't always agree in everything, but at least then we have the chance to talk things through and I find that always helps as well!

Gilly, I have a gut feeling about the Mafia Gangs, and I just do not like it, I feel that those down South are trying their best to manipulate trouble within all the various Mafia Gangs to make sure there will be this massive explosion!

The only reason for all of this is jealousy which is I think down to Robertson-Fox who is causing all this noise, but what we can do just does not bare thinking about! Some how he needs removing from this world!

It will not happen if MI6 have anything to do with it, as they have already failed twice last year! We need someone within the section to take out Robertson-Fox, because if he uses his evil way and manages to murder Toni, the all hell will be let loose!

All the Mafia Gangs have endowed Toni with the same Aura as Ken had for them, which does say a lot! In the eyes of all the Mafia Gangs neither Ken nor Toni his son can do any wrong!

The fact that Robertson-Fox is a twin of Ken's certainly complicates matters and certainly muddies the water, shall we say! But why keep it hidden for all these years? No wonder Robertson-Fox was always standing up at Westminster and nit-picking about Ken's daughter who was in charge of the Mafia Gangs at that particular time!

If Robertson-Fox had met her in the corridor's of Westminster he would have murdered her on the very spot!

Gilly any progress with Benedict's funeral, nearly complete Millie, as you know there had to be a Post Mortem carried out, and then that was delivered to the Coroner. Calm down Gilly, you
don't have to inform me what is happening, although I would have thought there would have to be an inquest!

Millie, you just stopped me from saying all of that, yes there is going to be an inquest in that the Coroner states that he was murdered by people unknown! Therefore while I was there he suggested that the Police had let them down and that a case should be open at once and certain enquiries are being made now.

What I do not understand is why they were not started once the body was found, yes Gilly and I cannot believe they did not start it straight away, in fact I tell you what to say but do it as from Gilly Penworth Murder Investigations.

Contact the Chief Constable, and use these words Gilly, nothing different just use these:-

I Gilly Penworth Murder Investigations, would like to make a point in court and ask why the Police did not start a murder enquiry when someone was murdered on the Carlisle-Settle Train! Further more I would like to know why the passengers on that same train were allowed to go about their business, when they should have been kept on that train, whilst the Police had taken down statements from all the passengers!

It would appear that the Police have been entirely lax in their duty to the person's family, in that no enquiry was started and indeed still as not been started.

I would like to know why the Police were so lax in their duty to the person who was murdered and indeed to the family of the murdered person!

Perhaps after you have had a public enquiry as to why this has been allowed to happen, you would have the courtesy of writing to me with all the necessary details of the enquiry!

I feel that the Police have no looked on this murder case as a serious matter, and consequently they lost the chance of ever apprehending anyone for this murder!

I sincerely hope that no one within the Government interfered with the investigation which should have been started straight away! I have a feeling that someone who is sitting in Westminster while I am speaking you, as been allowed to sway the Police away from having a public enquiry. I know why that is, it is purely due to the fact that he knew that the deceased was coming to have a meeting within my Office and was due to deliver certain information which would have ended the career of this particular Chap and also have him sentenced for the murder that you have never bothered to hold an enquiry into for whatever reason.

Unless I hear back from you within the next twenty-four hours, I shall formally request a full Police enquiry regarding the lack of activity within the Police with regard to this murder and also a Public enquiry into this murder that has not been looked into at all!

I also formally request that the Chief Constable telephone me as soon as he reads this note, signed Millie and Gilly Penworth Murder Investigations!

Gilly are you there, yes Millie well your 'phone is ringing yes I know and I have an awful feeling that it could be the Chief Constable, well in that case, but the call on open and then we can both listen to him and speak as and when we want! Yes that is a good idea!

Gilly Penworth, Good Morning, Chief Constable here, is Millie available, yes we both are, I will turn it over to double speak then we can all speak together! Right fire away!

Well why are you trying to tell me how the Police should act for a start! That is easy, because I would like to know why the Police did not do their duty, in that nothing was carried out with regard to the murder which was carried out on the Carlisle-Settle Train!

1. None of the passengers were kept on the Train until any statements had been given by any of the passengers direct to the Police, indeed no passengers were ever asked if they would give a statement to the Police!
2. Why were all passengers allowed to leave the Train when a murder had just taken place on that Train, without giving their names and addresses to the Police who were standing around the Train?
3. Why did the Police totally ignore that the murderer had shot the victim, and also stabbed him. What we call a Belt and Braces Job! They could see that the chap had been brutally murdered! No doubt about this being a murder at all!
4. Now why was this particular murder swept away as quickly as possible by the Police, there was no

consideration given to the murder victims family, was there!

5. This whole situation as been tried to be covered up by the Yorkshire Police, and as I have always worked well with the Yorkshire Police throughout my career, I am extremely cross to see your Police letting the side down!
6. Further I do not believe for a second that the Police have let down anyone, I believe that this as been caused by a certain person who sits down in Westminster and steals his monies from the Government for warming his bum on a chair so many hours in the week when the Government is sitting, and then he comes home and does bugger all.
7. This time he has certainly come a cropper as they say in Yorkshire, as he as interfered in the running of a Yorkshire Police Force.
8. I will let you have his name in a second, but all our 'phones are special and I would like to opening speak with this Chap and you can all hear what I will say to him and hopefully he will answer my questions, and I want you to keep dead quiet until I ask if you have anything to say. Will that be all right with you both? Yes Millie, are we in for a bit of a shock Millie? no not really I have been saying all this since the Murder but no one in authority as seen to act accordingly, so I have decided Gilly and I will run with it!
9. BUT AND IT IS CERTAINLY A BIG BUT – the Yorkshire Police must act immediately I accuse them of Murder. You need to ask the Police in Westminster to be on red alert for a call from you, the second after I have called the Chap an out and out murderer, I will give you time to set the police side in motion, this is incredibly serious.
10. Now the name of the Chap I shall call to his face that he as murdered various people ,is Sir Marcus Henry Robertson-Fox! He as been allowed to hide in Westminster for the last twenty-five years.
11. From this day forward I hope he will receive from the Court the death sentence for all his nasty ways

12. Millie are you completely sure of the facts, yes you see he is thinking that because he has murdered this particular person, then he is in the clear, what he does not know is that just before the chap was murdered he had a funny feeling about Robertson-Fox and signed a Statement of truth! Which I received via registered post!
13. Shall Gilly and I start the Patch phone working, are you both comfortable with this method, yes Millie if you are sure you can carry it out. Oh, we know we can but what I am worried about is your side of it, You need to warn the people in Westminster that we are going to arrest a member of the House for murder and they need to be standing in there so that when I accuse them of the murder he will try and make a run for it, as he is a coward even though his twin was the Leader of all the Mafia Gangs!
14. You need your Police in Westminster to be able to make an arrest in seconds of me saying

to Robertson-Fox that he murdered Benedict on the Train! Can you make sure that your Men down in Westminster will not tip him off about the coming arrest and that they should be in civvies so he does not get alerted to the fact that police are in the chambers!

15. Hello, put me onto the Police in Westminster ,yes Yorkshire Police, the matter is extremely urgent! Hello yes, we have to arrest a member of Parliament, it must be carried out swiftly but the Member of Parliament must not know anything about this matter until the Police have their handcuffs out to arrest him! Do you understand how serious this matter is? Yes. I Will give you the name of the MP when you have spoken direct to the Chief Constable of North Yorkshire.
16. Right all spoken to Millie, now you give the Police in Westminster the name of the Member of Parliament they have to arrest and bring up here! The name of the murderer is Sir Marcus Henry Robertson-Fox he carried out the murder of Mr. Benedict also a member of the House, whilst he was travelling on the Carlisle-Settle

Train, he then shot him and stabbed him, as you would expect him to do, as he is the twin brother of Ken who was the Head of all the Mafia Gangs, and I think what made him do this was the fact that Toni, who is now the Head of all the Mafia Gangs was appointed and not Robertson-Fox, incidentally he received the title from his grandfather as he was born 7 Minutes before Ken!

17. I think I had better patch the phone to Westminster and speak with Robertson-Fox! Yes could you patch to Sir Marcus Henry Robertson-Fox please, yes I am, no please do not alert him just put me via the patch. Thank you! Hello, is that Sir Robertson-Fox yes it is, who is that please, my name is Millie Aveyard, I have some news for you which I thought I should let you know about before anyone else could, well fire away. Are you sat down, yes of course I am bloody sat down I am in Westminster!

18. I would like to say, that you are being arrested for the murder of Mr. Benedict, whose murder you carried out on the Carlisle-Settle Train! Further more you carried out this murder so that certain information was not given out by Mr. Benedict!

19. I have to inform you that you carried out this murder far too late as Mr. Benedict had already posted the information direct to me.

20. Now Gentlemen have you arrested him. Yes Mam he is handcuffed! Then send him down and let us hope he gets the death sentence, as he certainly deserves it!

21. Actually is there anything you would like to say with regard to the murder you have carried out, no only that I should have done it years ago! Yes but you would never have been in charge of all the Mafia Gangs, it would always have gone to Ken's Children! How do you know about that? When your Brother Ken did his training for Pathology my Professor Hall and I, helped him!

22. That is why I hated him, he was always getting help. Well don't you get help in Westminster! Take him down please gentlemen before he asks for help!

23. Now Gilly would you like to take this murder case

forward, and make sure that Robertson-Fox is not given any special treatment in prison, because he may well ask for special treatment because he has been a member of parliament for twenty-five years now at least!

Let me know what your charges are Gilly and then I will make sure you are not kept waiting at all! You are good to me! Do you know Millie I cannot believe that chap just accepted the Police taking him down!

I just wondered if he had something up his sleeve. I think he will either manage to get loose or he will kill himself in his cell.

Get me the Chief Constable please, hello Millie here, could you make a point of 'phoning the Police down at Westminster or should I say who ever their Boss is, and make sure that Robertson-Fox does not have a gun or tablets to make a way out for him, such as Suicide!. We just have a feeling that he was too willing to be arrested, therefore we think he will attempt suicide, Please keep an alert out on him.

I will call them straight away Millie, and then call you back. Many thanks! Hi Millie,They have done a strip and took some tablets from him, these are being looked at, and they will come back when they know exactly what they are and we will let you know! OK, many thanks for that!

Hello Millie speaking, who is that, Me Millie, Gilly what are you doing on an open line? Simple really because all our patched lines and private 'phones have been tapped! When I say our I mean Gilly Penworth Murder Investigations! I think it must have something to do with Robertson-Fox! In fact I would put money on it Millie, yes Gilly and so would I!

Contact the chief Constable Gilly, and tell him all that as been thrown at you and I since Robertson-Fox was sent to Prison! Then ask him to have a word with the MI6 Boys and we require all services to be back to normal within the next 20 minutes! Will they reconnect them Millie so quick? Well if not I shall want to know why!

Hello Gilly Penworth speaking, well good morning Gilly, what are you doing on an outside line< well Millie and I believe the fact that all our private lines together with the Patch lines are once again rendered useless; can be traced back to Robertson-Fox, this is the fourth time in the last three months!

Ever since Millie had a 'phone call from Mr. Benedict, which was his first call to her in over two years. We know that Robertson-Fox was keeping surveillance on Benedict, that is how he knew about Mr. Benedict's phone calls to Millie, and the arranged meeting in Settle!

With Robertson-Fox knowing all what was going on with Mr. Benedict and Millie, he was in a position so he thought to arrange for the murder of Mr. Benedict, he simply had a belt and braces job done on Mr. Benedict, A typical Mafia Murder in fact!

Robertson-Fox is pure evil personified, he really is! Robertson-Fox's own nephew became the leader of the whole of the Mafia Gangs Worldwide, so what does Robertson-Fox do? He only starts complaining that he should have been asked to be the Leader of all the Mafia Gangs!

When he was politely told to get lost, what did he do, he decided to murder Benedict because that way he made sure that no one was keeping a check on what all the Mafia Gangs around the World were doing or even just thinking of doing!

I firmly believe that he was responsible for the murder of the Leader of the Mafia Gangs and that murder lead to Toni being appointed! Toni being the Leader, is as it should be as he is one of Ken's sons.

There is something slightly strange about the relationship between Toni, Robertson-Fox and Ken! Robertson-Fox a couple of weeks ago, started a story going around about Robertson-Fox and Ken being Twins, and that he was born seven minutes earlier than Ken, also the seven minutes between them allowed Robertson-Fox to inherit his Grandfather's Title!

Ken was never bothered about the various Titles, as all he wanted in the end was to rule the Worldwide Mafia Gangs, which he did! So now his own son is in charge and doing a good job so I am told!

It appears that Toni is running the ship as tight as Ken always did! He was told by Robertson-Fox that he would take over control of half of the Mafia Gangs, as he would help Toni to lead the Gangs!

The word is that Toni was quite verbal in reply, but basically he was told to keep his nose out of all Mafia affairs, as he knew absolutely nothing about the Mafia or how it was run and further more, Toni's father had left a small trust fund for Robertson-Fox which as paid off the mortgage he had on his Flat near Westminster and his House in Scotland, he as his salary as a Member of Parliament and a trust fund that Ken set up for him many years ago.

Robertson-Fox is a lazy chap, in fact he is bone idle, as they say in Yorkshire, he is work shy! And that is one thing you cannot say about his twin – called Ken!

You might not agree with Ken and his Mafia Operations, but he looked after all those that worked for him! If any of the family had a problem, he was there sorting everything out, so that once again everything was running like clock work!

The Mafia Gangs are being pulled towards a massive explosion and that is when various Mafia Groups try and take over smaller Mafia Gangs!

For instance The Russian Mafia is against the Dutch Mafia Gang for how they operate with Europe! The Mexico Mafia are upsetting a few of the Mafia Gangs by the way they sell their wares around the world!

The United States Mafia is trying to muscle their way into Europe! The Ialian Mafia is proud of Toni, the Leader of all the Mafia Gangs! Although it as been talked about quite openly that some Mafia Gangs are resentful about Toni being appointed by his Father as overall Leader!

Toni's Father appointed him and he should be allowed to continue until he dies! Exactly like all the other Leaders have done! It as been talked about in the various Gangs that Toni will be murdered and then someone else will be appointed.

I hope the death of Mr. Benedict will cause something to happen with the Halls of Westminster because with Mr. Benedict's murder by Robertson-Fox and by Robertson-Fox buying certain members of MI5 and MI6 who knows what they are planning against the various Mafia Gangs.

The Government would be better advised to actually do nothing at the moment, and see exactly what is waiting in the wings!

      The Mafia Gangs are certainly earning a fair amount of monies all around the World! Simply due to the way Ken organised them all, and Toni, if left to do the Job his Father gave to him, will continue in the same way as his Father worked!

      I would feel more comfortable Gilly, if Robertson-Fox was not hiding in the background, because of the grumbles about having Toni as the Leader of all the Mafia Gangs! That moan was started on the instructions of Robertson-Fox, just because he thought if enough of the various Gangs would agree with him, then he would be able to push his nephew to one side, and then he, Robertson-Fox would take over at the Leader of all the Mafia Gangs! He tried and eventually struck lucky in carrying out a full Mafia Murder on Mr. Benedict!

      What Robertson-Fox forgot was that Mr. Benedict had been in Government for quite a number of years, and kept his nose to the ground, he always seemed very well informed by both sides of the Government, so much so that when he visited Scotland, he thought Robertson-Fox might try and so something, and he was convinced he was being tailed, as indeed he was as Sir Marcus Henry Robertson-Fox had organised for him to be tailed when he left Westminster!

      What Robertson-Fox did not know was that Benedict was visiting Scotland so they could collate the turnover figures for all the Mafia Gangs who work within Scotland.

      Benedict has always said he thought it was high in relation to the size of Scotland, but he was totally amazed that the combined yearly turnover for all Mafia Gangs in Scotland amounts to a turnover of 33 Billion Pounds!

      After Benedict received this information, he telephoned me and arranged to meet with me in Skipton but knew that Robertson-Fox would work out who he might visit, so cancelled our meeting in Skipton and we arranged to meet in Settle!

      Benedict had a Tip-off that Robertson-Fox had put out a price on Benedict being murdered and the rest you know! Although as usual Benedict was one step ahead, as before they got too close to Benedict he managed to send me a Registered Package full of his evidence against Robertson-Fox and his dealing in connection with MI5 and MI6 and also the price he had put on Benedict Murder!

Gilly as taken over the case against Robertson-Fox and she is well into the contents of all the proof regarding Robertson-Fox together with some people within MI5 and MI6 being involved, actually being paid cash backhanders, for informing Robertson-Fox what exactly Benedict was organising and who he 'phoned! Also so who he met face to face!

More important to Robertson-Fox was the names of the various people he would 'phone and arrange to see during his travels around the world!

Westminster operates just like a small city, probably similar in fact to The Vatican and with the same type of intrigue and petty jealousy! With murder and greed all thrown into the Mix!

With Mr. Benedict knowing what the Ringleaders in Westminster were hoping to do, and the input of MI6 being common knowledge, he admitted his time was running out, he had got to be 84 years old, although his true age of 84 years old was certainly not common knowledge.

Yes we all knew he was part of the fittings of Westminster and had been working there for a great number of years, but never knew his real age until Robertson-Fox murdered him!

What we are left with now is one hell of a mess created by Robertson-Fox and his servants in MI5 and MI6, as Robertson-Fox used all the monies in his Trust Fund that his brother Ken made for him so he could pay cash backhanders to personnel from MI5 and MI6 to tip him off about Mr. Benedict!

Robertson-Fox was paying out cash to MI5 and MI6 so he was informed of all the Prime Minister movements, together with Benedict's movement. Plus of course he received movements that Millie was carrying out as she has and will always have top level cover because of the work she does now and as done for years with Professor Hall. Those three are the only ones with top cover at all times!

Robertson-Fox is so jealous of Millie, that he as had her cover stopped together with all patched lines tampered with, he is penniless at this moment because he has paid for all this to be carried out, and hopefully once everything is formulated, Robertson-Fox and his Cronies from the Government will be sent to prison for life!

I just hope that the whole sordid mess will be allowed to come out in Court, and yes I do realise that the Court will be closed, but at least I would hear , all the dirty dealings between Robertson-Fox and his cronies in both MI5 and MI6 can be made known in Court, which it should be.

When that devil is in Court the sentence should be life in prison, which I believe he will receive, and that should be the same for the Black Suits as well. The judge will certainly come down heavily on members of the Government of the day when they try and hide behind their powers of Government!

I feel we have done a good job on Mr. Benedict's behalf and hope he can rest in peace now! The Court will now deal with all the necessary paperwork which will be required, and very soon we shall have a good result on Mr. Benedict's behalf!

Gilly are you up-to-date with the Murder case for Mr. Benedict? Yes Millie but we cannot conclude everything until the Court Case is over with regard to Robertson-Fox , then there is the Murder case regarding Mr. Benedict.

Millie, we can only conclude our side of things once all the Court cases have finished, and then we are free to bring our own cases. If we try and bring our cases forward, we shall not be fully prepared!

I think everything will be finalised within the next few days, so do not start worrying about something, that may not happen! Yes Gilly you are right, I will keep quiet, well if you do it will be a first Millie.

Millie I am listing all our cases which we have in waiting regarding Mr.Benedict and his Friends down South.

1. Case for the Murder of Mr. Benedict which was ordered on the instructions of Robertson-Fox.
2. Case for the attempted Murder of staff of Gilly Penworth Murder Investigations including Millie! Which was ordered on the instructions of

Robertson-Fox.
3. Case for the attempted murder of Gilly Penworth, together with her cousin Milly and all her family, plus the interference with all her Government Equipment and Telephone lines, and her home being broken into.
4. Case for the attempted Burglary at Millie's new home, which was supposed to be kept a secret but MI5 and MI6 were leaking like a sieve!
5. Case brought against certain members of a Government Department regarding the matter of breaking and entry into Millie's Estate. Plus damaging all 'phone lines including the hot line direct from MI6 and MI5 which in the 30 years Millie has been using these, there had never been a problem. The damage was caused on the instructions of Robertson-Fox..

    I think that will do for now Millie, because it could be a year before they go into Court. The main think is we now know the culprit and he is in prison, they have him on a suicide watch, so that should mean he will not be able to take his own life.
    So I would say Millie, that the job is done, Mr. Benedict can rest in peace, and I think we both have done well. We may never have to take our cases into Court as they could become part and parcel of the Main Cases brought against Robertson-Fox. That could work out better and quicker for all concerned!
    Anyway the outcome as been good, The Murderer was in Prison in record time, The various Government Departments are now been looked at very carefully indeed. I think we can give ourselves a pat on the back, Millie! No do not do that you will only tempt fate Gilly!

!

Printed in Great Britain
by Amazon